914.7

World in Focus
Russia

ROB BOWDEN AND GALYA RANSOME

WAYLAND

First published in 2007 by Wayland, an imprint of Hachette Children's Books

Hachette Children's Books, 338 Euston Road, London NW1 3BH

Wayland Australia, Hachette Children's Books, Level 17/207 Kent Street, Sydney, NSW 2000

Commissioning editor: Nicola Edwards
Editor: Patience Coster
Inside design: Chris Halls, www.mindseyedesign.co.uk
Cover design: Wayland
Series concept and project management by EASI-Educational Resourcing (info@easi-er.co.uk)
Statistical research: Anna Bowden
Maps and graphs: Martin Darlison, Encompass Graphics

Printed in China

British Library Cataloguing in Publication Data
Ransome, Galya
    Russia. - (World in focus)
    1. Russia (Federation) - Juvenile literature
    I. Title II. Bowden, Rob
    947'.086

ISBN-13: 978-0-7502-4740-5

Cover top: The Winter Palace in St Petersburg was once home to the tsars of Imperial Russia, but is now best known as part of the world famous Hermitage museum.
Cover bottom and title page: Russian children light candles during a Christmas ceremony at a church in the village of Zhilino, near Moscow.

The authors and publisher would like to thank the following for allowing their pictures to be reproduced in this publication: Corbis 4 (Pascal Le Segretain), 5 (Sergei Chirikov), 6 (Barry Lewis), 8 (Alfredo Dagli Orti), 9 (Bettmann), 10 (Bettmann), 11 (David Mdzinarishvili), 12 (Gianni Giansanti), 13 (Peter Blakely), 14 (Staffan Widstrand), 15 (Yann Arthus-Bertrand), 16 (Wolfgang Kaehler), 17 (Alexander Demianchuk), 18 (Robert Wallis), 19 (Gideon Mendel), 20 (Paul A. Souders), 21 (Morton Beebe), 22 (Sergei Karpukhin), 23 (Sergei Karpukhin), 24 (Reuters), 25 (Reuters), 26 (Alexander Natruskin), 27 (Shepard Sherbell), 28 Peter Turnley, 29 Maria Golovnina, 30 Sergie Chirikov, 31 Abraham Nowitz, 32 (Alexander Natruskin), 33 (Peter MacDiarmid), 34 (Yuri Kochetkov), 35 (Hulton-Deutsch Collection), 36 (Li Gang), 37 (Reuters), 38 (Geoff Arrow), 39 (Steve Raymer), 40 Buddy Mays, 41 Richard T. Nowitz, 42 Gideon Mendel, 43 Gideon Mendel, 44 (Savintsev Fyodor/ITAR-TASS), 45 (Gideon Mendel), 46 (Stephen Hird), 47 (Le Segretain/Corbis Sygma), 48 and *title page* (Reuters/Viktor Korotayev), 49 (Michel Setboun), 50 (Richard Klune), 51 (Dean Conger), 52 (Gidcon Mendel), 53 (Steve Raymer), 54 (Robert Wallis), 55 (Vladimir Smolyakov), 56 (Gleb Garanich), 57 (Reuters), 58 (Sergei Chirikov), 59 (Dima Korotayev).

The directional arrow portrayed on the map on page 7 provides only an approximation of north.

The data used to produce the graphics and data panels in this title were the latest available at the time of production.

CONTENTS

CHAPTER 1

Russia – An Overview

Russia is the world's largest country, stretching from Europe in the west to the Asia-Pacific in the east. It is also one of the world's most powerful countries, possessing great natural wealth and playing an important role in world politics.

A CENTURY OF CHANGE

The twentieth century was a turbulent time for Russia. At the beginning of the century, the country was ruled by the autocratic Tsar Nicholas II, the last of the Romanov tsars (see page 9), but in 1917 the people revolted against him. The revolution ushered in the rise of communism under the leadership of Vladimir Lenin, and in 1922 the Union of Soviet Socialist Republics (USSR) emerged as the world's first communist state.

Russia was by far the most dominant republic within the USSR, and Moscow became the new Soviet capital (prior to the 1917 revolution, the Russian capital had been St Petersburg). There followed several decades of rapid industrialization and economic growth, but the Soviet era was marred by violence against anyone who spoke out against authority, and millions of people died as a result. When the Germans invaded Russia during the Second World War, the USSR was drawn into the conflict and sided with the Allied forces to defeat the Nazi regime. By the end of the war in 1945, the USSR had seized control of large areas of eastern Europe and instilled communist principles into many of their governments. Politically the world was divided, between communism in the east and

► A tourist boat travels along the Moscow River towards the Great Kremlin Palace and the Kremlin's cathedrals. Once the powerhouse of the Soviet empire (the USSR), the Kremlin is now the seat of Russia's democratically elected president.

◀ Despite its troubles, Russia has retained its position, alongside the USA, as the major player in manned space flight. This photo shows a Soyuz rocket being prepared for a mission to the international space station in March 2006.

democracy in the west. A so-called 'Cold War' followed, in which the USSR and the USA were the world's two superpowers and they regarded each other with intense hostility and suspicion.

In the mid 1970s, the economy of the USSR began to falter and intellectuals within the country began to speak out against communism. Despite attempts by the Communist Party to reverse this process and silence its critics, the situation worsened and by the early 1980s the USSR was in crisis. The Soviet leader, Mikhail Gorbachev attempted to introduce radical new reforms after coming to power in 1985, but these were too little and came too late. At the end of 1991, the USSR had become so fragmented that Russia and other Soviet states declared themselves as independent republics.

NEW BEGINNINGS

During the last decade of the twentieth century, Russia underwent dramatic reforms in an attempt to move away from its communist past

and align itself with the free-market economies and democratic political systems that are found in many countries of the world. Russia benefited by inheriting the USSR's immense natural resources (including oil, gas, coal, timber and numerous minerals), its educated and skilled workforce, and its status in global politics. However, Russia also inherited many problems, including a culture of corruption and bribery and an environment ravaged by years of careless industrialization. There are also political problems, such as factions within Russia (especially in the republic of Chechnya) that seek further autonomy or even independence from Moscow.

Today, in the twenty-first century, the signs are more positive. Russia's economy is growing, corruption has been reduced and political tensions in the regions are being resolved, although this is a slow process. Poverty remains high, however, and life expectancy is lower than it was under the USSR. The Russian president, Vladimir Putin, has the firm backing of the population and was re-elected with more than 70 per cent of the vote in the elections of March 2004. Putin intends to bring in further sweeping reforms that will turn Russia into a major world economy. He has already shown his commitment to such pledges, building closer political and economic ties with Europe and the USA to the west, and China and Japan to the east. Despite these positive signs, analysts think it is too early to say whether Russia has completed the most difficult part of its transformation into a major world democracy.

Did you know?

The city of Kaliningrad (formerly Königsberg) on the Baltic coast became part of Russia at the end of the Second World War. The area was separated from the main part of Russia in the early 1990s when Lithuania and Belarus became independent. Today it remains a Russian enclave, strategically important for its access to the Baltic Sea.

Physical geography

- Land area: 16,995,800 sq km/6,562,085 sq miles
- Water area: 79,400 sq km/30,656 sq miles
- Total area: 17,075,200 sq km/6,592,741 sq miles
- World rank (by area): 1
- Land boundaries: 20,017 km/12,438 miles
- Border countries: Azerbaijan, Belarus, China, Estonia, Finland, Georgia, Kazakhstan, North Korea, Latvia, Lithuania, Mongolia, Norway, Poland, Ukraine
- Coastline: 37,653 km/23,397 miles
- Highest point: Mount Elbrus (5,642 m/ 18,510 ft)
- Lowest point: Caspian Sea (-28 m/-92 ft)

Source: CIA World Factbook

Did you know?

Russia is so vast that its territory from east to west crosses 11 time zones.

▶ People out walking in Moscow's snow-covered Gorky Park.

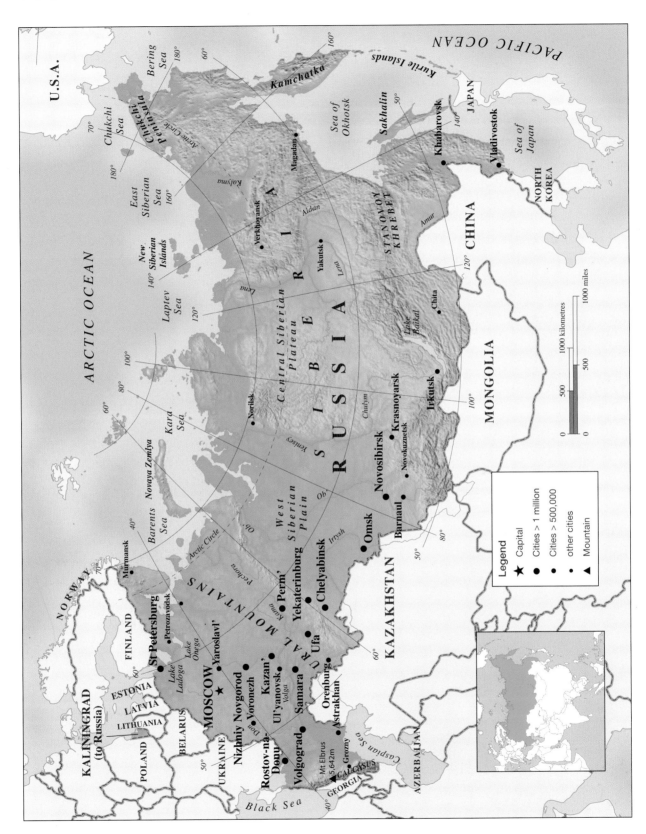

CHAPTER 2

History

Russia has one of the most complex histories of any nation, influenced both by events in Europe and Asia and by the country's own ever-changing boundaries during years of expansion and contraction.

EARLY HISTORY

People have occupied parts of Russia since the second millennium BC, but little is known about these early settlers. Rather more reliable history dates from the sixth century AD, when a people called the Slavs occupied parts of eastern and central Europe. Several tribes of eastern Slavs appear to have been the first Slavs to settle in the lands that are now Russia. A possibly legendary account suggests that, in about the ninth century, some of these Slavs were ruled by Prince Rurik, a Viking warrior. The Vikings quickly integrated with the Slavs and formed a state known as Rus (there is some debate about whether this name came from the Vikings or the Slavs) with a capital in Kiev (today the capital of Ukraine). Kiev became an important trading centre with trade routes extending north to the Baltic and south to the Black Sea. Besides trade, these routes also had an influence on society and culture. Christianity, for example, came to Russia through trade links with Constantinople (modern-day Istanbul) in around 982 during the reign of Vladimir, grand prince of Kiev.

In the thirteenth century Russia, like much of Asia, came under the control of Mongol Tatars led by Genghis Khan. The Mongol invasion signalled the demise of Kiev and, by the time Mongol rule ended in the early fifteenth century, a new centre of power had emerged – Moscow. The void left by the collapse of Mongol Tatar rule resulted in a series of conflicts being fought between Russian princes. Vasily II finally secured the Moscow throne in 1447 and began to consolidate power over other regions of Russia. The relative peace was short-lived, however, and internal wars and political struggles continued until the early seventeenth century, when the Romanov family came to the throne.

FROM EMPIRE TO REVOLUTION

The Romanov tsars oversaw a period of Russian empire building, during which the borders of control were expanded into new territories. However, the Russian empire was slow to develop economically and politically,

◀ A portrait of Peter the Great, tsar of Russia from 1682 to 1725 and one of the main figures in the period of Russian empire building.

Focus on: The last tsar

In 1917, Tsar Nicholas II abdicated and was imprisoned in Tobolsk in north-west Russia with his wife, Alexandra, their four daughters and their son. Not content with his fall from power, the communist revolutionary Bolsheviks who had seized control of Russia decided that the tsar had to die. In July 1918, Nicholas II and his family were executed in the house of a Yekaterinburg merchant. So bitter was the feeling against the royal family that their bodies were doused in acid, burned and thrown into a mine shaft. In 1970 their remains were discovered and eventually recovered in 1991. DNA tests conducted against living relatives of the Romanov family proved the remains were genuine, and in 1998 the family was buried alongside other members of the Romanov family in St Petersburg. In 2000, Tsar Nicholas II and his family were canonized (officially declared to be saints) by the Russian Orthodox Church.

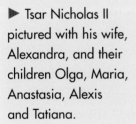 ► Tsar Nicholas II pictured with his wife, Alexandra, and their children Olga, Maria, Anastasia, Alexis and Tatiana.

and this led to considerable discontent among its subjects. In 1861, this discontent led Tsar Alexander II to abolish existing patterns of land ownership under which most Russian peasants had been living virtually as serfs. This gesture proved too little, however, and members of a revolutionary movement began to plan ways in which they might overthrow the royal family. In 1881, after several attempts, revolutionary terrorists assassinated Tsar Alexander II, but failed to overthrow the monarchy.

The successor to the throne, Tsar Alexander III, managed to resist the revolutionaries until his death in 1894, upon which his son, Nicholas II, came to power. Tsar Nicholas II was a weak ruler, heavily influenced by his wife, Alexandra Fyodorovna and a Siberian monk called Grigory Rasputin. Nicholas II had an opportunity to pacify the revolutionaries by turning Russia into a modern constitutional monarchy, with an elected parliament and the tsar as head of state. A parliament was established, but in reality it had few powers.

Nicholas II remained in control of the country and of the Russian army. The First World War had a disastrous economic effect on Russia and led to widespread discontent, which expressed itself in a series of workers' strikes that began in 1915 and became progressively bigger and more political. A turning point came in January 1917, when the army was sent in to Moscow to disperse workers who were calling for an end to the power and domination of the tsar. The army refused to obey orders and joined the workers in calling for change, and their example was soon followed in other parts of Russia. In February 1917 the Duma (Russian parliament) formed a provisional government to try to restore social order, but it was weak and failed to bring stability. In the same month Tsar Nicholas II was forced to abdicate his throne, bringing the 300-year rule of the Romanov dynasty to an end.

THE DAWN OF COMMUNISM

In October 1917 the Bolshevik Party, under its leader Vladimir Lenin, overthrew the provisional government and seized control of St Petersburg. However, the Bolsheviks did not have immediate control over the vast lands of Russia and a bitter civil war erupted, in which Lenin and his Red Army gradually crushed any opposition. The war ended in 1921.

The following year saw the formation of the Union of Soviet Socialist Republics (USSR) or Soviet Union, the world's first communist state. Under communism, almost all aspects of life were brought under the central control of the ruling Communist Party. This model would later be followed by others and became the basis of the Cold War between those countries supporting communism and those supporting democracy (see pages 11-12).

Lenin's death in 1924 led to yet another power struggle in the leadership of the country. Two of the main contenders for this were Leon Trotsky, who had helped lead the Red Army during the civil war, and the general secretary of the Communist Party, Joseph Stalin. They and others disagreed on key policies about the future of the USSR, but Stalin's influence eventually triumphed and his power became absolute by the late 1920s. He is remembered as

▼ Vladimir Lenin, the Russian communist leader addresses a mass meeting in a Moscow square around 1920. Lenin asked the Russian people to remain united during what were turbulent times.

a ruthless leader who led the country through a period of rapid industrialization. He also supervised the reorganization of Soviet agriculture into state controlled 'collective farms'. Those who opposed Stalin risked persecution and death and it is claimed that as many as 25 million people died during his 'reign of terror'.

At the outbreak of the Second World War Stalin agreed a pact of non-aggression with Nazi Germany which enabled the USSR to take control of Latvia, Lithuania, Estonia and half of Poland. However, after German forces invaded Russia in 1941, Stalin joined the Allies against the Nazis. Once involved, the Soviet forces were engaged in some of the war's most ferocious battles and an estimated 25 million Soviet citizens were killed. The Soviet involvement proved vital in the eventual overthrow of the Nazis and was to have repercussions for the next half century.

After the Second World War ended, Europe begain to rebuild itself. The Soviet Union remained in control of much of eastern Europe, and a political divide emerged between communist governments of the east and the democratic governments of the west. This political division became known as the 'Iron Curtain' and was symbolized by the construction of the Berlin Wall, which divided the German city into a democratic sector (West Berlin) and a communist sector (East Berlin). As these divides became more apparent, a new type of war emerged. The Cold War focused not on physical conflict but on military threats and the building of huge stores of nuclear weapons to intimidate the opposing side. Technological superiority became another important aspect of the Cold War, most evident

▲ Joseph Stalin was a brutal Soviet dictator, but his memory is honoured here by a loyal Georgian communist who carries the leader's portrait to mark the 53rd anniversary of his death (in March 1953).

 Did you know?

In 1962, the Soviet premier Nikita Khrushchev (leader 1953-64) brought the world to the brink of nuclear war. He provided the USSR's communist ally, Cuba, with nuclear weapons to protect itself from possible attack by the USA. This led to a tense stand-off between the USSR and USA (under President John F. Kennedy). This eventually ended with the USSR withdrawing nuclear weapons from Cuba in return for a promise from the USA never to invade the communist country.

in the 'space race' between the USSR and the USA. In 1957 the USSR succeeded in launching the first satellite and in 1961 became the first nation to launch a manned space flight.

THE BEGINNING OF THE END

Despite the USSR's success in the space race, the communist system was failing to keep up with the demands of daily life. By the 1970s shops were often without goods, and queues formed for even basic supplies. At the same time the Soviet government began to lose its controlling grip on the the media and people became more aware of life beyond the Iron Curtain. The Communist Party faced growing criticism from intellectuals and some members of the wider population, and it reacted by imprisoning or deporting its critics.

By the early 1980s, the USSR was in crisis with further decline in the economy and its leadership increasingly out of touch with reality. An element of stability returned in 1985, when Mikhail Gorbachev became premier of the USSR. Gorbachev recognized the need for urgent economic and political reforms and introduced two new policies – of *perestroika* (a restructuring of politics and the economy) and *glasnost* (openness about political ideas and what was happening in the USSR). Despite ambitious plans, *perestroika* was poorly implemented, while *glasnost* strengthened the arguments of those already disillusioned with communism and the USSR. As discontent grew, several parts of the Soviet Union sought to break away from Moscow. In 1990, Gorbachev authorized the use of military force to try to keep the union intact. However, this further rallied people behind their individual republics and marked the beginning of the end for the USSR.

THE EMERGENCE OF RUSSIA

1991 was a fast-moving year in Soviet and Russian history. Boris Yeltsin, the newly elected president of Russia (at that point a republic within the USSR), emerged to challenge Gorbachev. Yeltsin argued for an independent Russia and an end to communism. In August 1991, he put down an attempted coup by communist hardliners, an event that greatly weakened Gorbachev's standing. Gorbachev remained in power, but Yeltsin became

▶ Soviet leader Mikhail Gorbachev was the architect of *glasnost* and *perestroika* – policies designed to save the troubled USSR. In the end, they brought about its demise.

► Vladimir Putin (centre, without a hat) visits the Tomb of the Unknown Soldier during the day of a homeland defender celebrations in 1999. Shortly afterwards he was elected president, in March 2000.

politically stronger and used his position to undermine Gorbachev's authority by banning the Communist Party in Russia and seizing all of its property. On 25 December 1991, Gorbachev resigned and, on 31 December, the USSR officially ceased to exist. Russia emerged from the fallen USSR as an independent republic with Boris Yeltsin as its president. Fourteen other former Soviet republics had also become independent nations.

RUSSIA SINCE 1991

Yeltsin inherited a declining economy and a country full of political and social tensions. The 1990s were plagued with problems including mass unemployment, rising poverty, growing crime and ethnic conflicts. Yeltsin pursued aggressive policies to try to drive through reforms. He also launched military action against a breakaway faction in the southern district of Chechnya. Under intense pressure, Yeltsin's health also began to deteriorate and he suffered a series of major heart attacks. By the

end of the 1990s Yeltsin had overseen a ceasefire in Chechnya. There were some signs of economic recovery, but Russia still faced an uphill struggle. In late 1999, Yeltsin resigned as president and appointed his young prime minister, Vladimir Putin, as his successor.

Under Putin, economic and political reforms continued apace. Some people believed these reforms handed too much control to the president and his appointed deputies, but others applauded Putin for attempting to stamp out corruption within the extensive political system. The economy has boomed under Putin's presidency and is bringing record levels of foreign revenue into Russia thanks to its vast energy reserves (see pages 26-7). Putin has also raised the profile of Russia in global affairs. He has become a well respected statesman, with firm opinions. Putin was against the manner in which the US led the invasion of Iraq for example, despite pledging his full support for the international war on terrorism.

CHAPTER 3

Landscape and Climate

Russia covers a vast area extending from the Baltic Sea in the west to the Pacific Ocean in the east and from the Arctic in the north to the Caspian Sea in the south. Covering 17,075,200 sq km (6,592,741 sq miles), Russia's area is almost twice that of the USA and nearly 70 times larger than the UK. Russia's immense size means that it includes a wide range of landscapes and experiences several different climates.

TUNDRA AND TAIGA

Much of Russia consists of vast and mainly flat plains. In the far north this landscape is known as tundra, a Russian term meaning 'treeless heights'. As its name suggests, the tundra is a treeless habitat with a generally harsh climate and extremely low winter temperatures of less than -30°C (-22°F). Beneath the surface of the tundra there is generally a layer of permanently frozen subsoil, called permafrost, which can be up to 1,400 m (4,593 ft) deep. The very harsh conditions mean that the tundra is dominated by lichens, mosses, grasses and small shrubs. South of the tundra lies the taiga, which is a forest covering most of northern and eastern Russia. The taiga also experiences a harsh climate, with long, cold winters and temperatures below freezing for at least six months of the year. Summers are short, warm

▼ A herd of reindeer (also known as caribou) grazes on the tundra plains of Siberia on the Chukchi Peninsula.

 An aerial view of the taiga landscape near Tjumen. Taiga (also known as boreal forest) covers much of northern and eastern Russia.

and wet, and at this time the forests thrive with insect and bird life. Besides coniferous tree species such as pine, spruce, larch and hemlock, the taiga vegetation is mainly mosses, lichens and grasses.

DIVIDING MOUNTAINS

Russia is split geographically by the Ural Mountains (Urals) that extend north to south for around 2,500 km (1,550 miles) and are traditionally considered the divide between Europe to the west and Asia to the east. The land to the east of the Urals as far as the Pacific Ocean is known as Siberia and comprises about two-thirds of Russia. Dominated by tundra and taiga, Siberia has a much lower population than other parts of Russia and is less developed.

Siberia is important to the Russian economy, however, as it is where the majority of Russia's mineral wealth is found (see page 29), especially in the northern regions. The Urals themselves are also rich in mineral resources and support a thriving industrial economy.

? Did you know?

The taiga biome (habitat) covers a greater area than any other land-based habitat. From Russia, the taiga extends into Scandinavia. It is also present in North America, where it is more commonly known as boreal forest.

Russia's other great dividing mountains are the Caucasus Mountains that run along Russia's southern border with Georgia and Azerbaijan. The mountains extend for around 1,200 km (750 miles) between the Black Sea in the west and the Caspian Sea in the east. The Russian portion of the Caucasus Mountains includes Mount Elbrus which at about 5,642 m (18,510 ft) is the highest peak in both Russia and Europe. The name Elbrus refers to the mountain's twin peaks, and the eastern summit is slightly lower than the western one.

LAKES AND RIVERS

The Volga River in western Russia is the longest in Europe at 3,530 km (2,194 miles). The Volga's course flows through the most populated region of Russia and around half the country's total population lives within its river basin. The Volga and its major tributary, the Kama River, are extensively used for human benefit with eleven hydro-electric power (HEP) stations and numerous artificial reservoirs used for water supply and irrigation.

The longest river in Russia is the Lena. It flows northwards through western Siberia for 4,400 km (2,734 miles) before discharging into the Arctic Ocean. The Lena's waters are not yet intensively used but have considerable HEP potential, several times that of the Volga.

Lake Baikal in eastern Russia is the world's deepest freshwater lake. It has a maximum depth of 1,742 m (5,715 ft) and contains a fifth of all of the world's surface freshwater. It is also the oldest freshwater lake, dating back 20-25

? Did you know?

The Volga River system is fed by a network of around 151,000 rivers and streams that have a total length of 574,536 km (357,000 miles). This makes it one of the world's largest river systems.

▼ A train on the Trans-Siberian Railway passes by Lake Baikal, the world deepest and oldest freshwater lake and site of great ecological importance.

million years and its uniqueness means it has earned classification and protection as a World Heritage site. Despite this status, the lake suffers pollution from surrounding industries that include a cellulose factory and a paper mill. In 1971 the government introduced policies to protect the lake, but pollution remains an issue.

CLIMATE

Russia's enormous territory means that its climate is incredibly varied. In the broadest terms, the northern latitudes are colder than the southern latitudes, but the entire country is prone to extremes of temperature and generally harsh weather conditions in the long, cold winter months. Summers are short and can be very hot in the south with temperatures reaching up to 40°C (104°F). The majority of Russia's people live in the central regions of European Russia, where conditions are more balanced and extremes of temperature less pronounced.

▲ A driver steers a carriage across Dvortsovaya Square in St Petersburg during a winter snowstorm.

The Caspian Sea

Russia is one of five countries sharing the waters of the Caspian Sea, the world's largest enclosed body of water. At 386,400 sq km (149,190 sq miles) in area, it is larger than Japan. The sea is famous for its sturgeon fish whose caviar (eggs) are a renowned delicacy and one of the world's most expensive foods. Around 80 per cent of global caviar supply comes from the Caspian Sea. The Caspian Sea also has considerable oil and gas reserves beneath the sea bed and surrounding shores. This mineral wealth is the cause of ongoing political disputes over territorial rights between Russia and the other countries (Kazakhstan, Turkmenistan, Iran and Azerbaijan) sharing the sea.

Temperature= ●   Precipitation= ▬

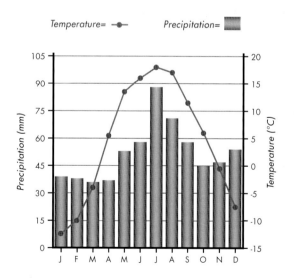

▲ Average monthly climate conditions in Moscow

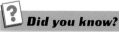
Did you know?

The lowest ever temperature in Russia was recorded in Verkhoyansk in 1933. It was -68°C or -90°F.

CHAPTER 4

Population and Settlements

Russia's population is dispersed across its vast territory and includes a diversity of ethnic groups with over 100 spoken languages. In global terms its 2005 population of 143.2 million people makes it the eighth most populous nation in the world.

POPULATION DECLINE

Up until 1989, the population of the then USSR had been steadily growing. In post-1989 Russia, however, the general pattern has been a gradual decline in population and this is a trend predicted to continue into the future. There are many contributing factors to this trend, such as the high mortality rate among Russian men. Work-related accidents, alcoholism and poor diet and healthcare are the main reasons given for this. The average male life expectancy at birth fell from 65 in 1988 to just 58.8 in 2003.

Poor healthcare in general means that the infant mortality rate (an important measure of healthcare) is higher in Russia (at 16 deaths per 1,000 live births) than in other developed nations such as the UK or USA, where it is 5 and 7 deaths per 1,000 live births respectively. The problem is especially acute in Russia's more remote regions, where infant mortality rates as a result of infectious diseases or pneumonia may be several times higher than those of the more developed western region.

Russia's maternal mortality rate is also high (around three times that of the UK or USA), and is often the result of complications that can occur during abortion procedures. In the Soviet Union during the twentieth century, poor contraceptive practice meant that abortion was often the main method of birth control. Even today, abortion rates in Russia remain among the highest in the world and contribute directly to the country's low birth rate.

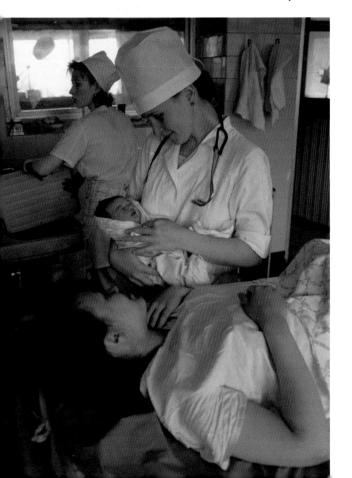

◀ A nurse cradles a newborn baby in a Moscow maternity hospital. Proper facilities such as this are helping to reduce Russia's relatively high maternal and infant mortality rates.

Some population experts predict that Russia's population decline could leave it with fewer than 100 million people by the middle of the twenty-first century. Under these circumstances it would be difficult to maintain a modern

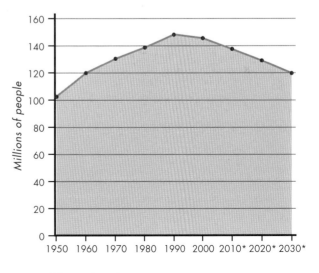

▲ At Bol'shoye Goloustnoye (near Lake Baikal) a boy takes the family cow to drink from a water hole. Russia's declining population could threaten rural livelihoods like this. The current generation is ageing and many younger people are moving to the cities.

Population data

- Population: 143.2 million
- Population 0-14 yrs: 16%
- Population 15-64 yrs: 70%
- Population 65+ yrs: 14%
- Population growth rate: - 0.6%
- Population density: 8.4 per sq km/21.7 per sq mile
- Urban population: 73%
- Major cities: Moscow   10,654,000
                 St Petersburg   5,312,000

Source: United Nations and World Bank

* Projected population

▲ Population growth, 1950-2030

developed economy in such a large country. Other experts believe that improvements in the economy and the standard of living, together with greater political stability and freedom, will encourage a return to positive population growth within this period. The impact of a declining population is being partially offset by migrants from former Soviet republics, many of whom are Russians or Russian speakers. The largest numbers of migrants are from Armenia, Azerbaijan, Georgia and Tajikistan.

ETHNIC DIVERSITY

Around 80 per cent of the people are ethnically Russian and only speak Russian. Among the remaining population of around 30 million there are more than 100 ethnic groups, some of which are very small and have languages that are almost extinct. All but the few groups living in remote areas speak Russian as well as their own language. The main ethnic minorities are Tatar (3.8 per cent), Ukrainian (2 per cent), Bashkir (1.2 per cent), Chuvash (1.1 per cent), Chechen (0.9 per cent) and Armenian (0.8 per cent).

DISTRIBUTION AND SETTLEMENT

Taken as a whole, Russia has a very low population density of just 8.4 people per sq km (21.7 per sq mile). This is almost four times lower than the USA and over 30 times lower than the UK. As so much of Russia's environment is hostile to human settlement, population distribution is far from even. In fact around 80 per cent of the population live in roughly 20 per cent of the land area in the central and southern parts of European Russia. In the Moscow region, population density is much higher than average, at around 140 people per sq km (360 per sq mile). In contrast, the Taymyr region of Siberia has a population density of just 0.05 people per sq km (0.11 per sq mile).

About 73 per cent of Russians live in urban areas. Moscow and St Petersburg are the major cities, with Moscow alone accounting for nearly 8 per cent of the population. Besides Moscow and St Petersburg, a further 11 cities have populations of between 1 and 2 million. Of these, only two, Omsk and Novosibirsk (both major industrial and transportation centres) are in Siberia.

► A Koryak grandmother and her granddaughter in a reindeer herding village in the Magadan region of north-east Russia. The Koryak are one of Russia's many ethnic minorities, with fewer than 9,000 members.

▲ An aerial view across Moscow, the largest city in Russia and one of the most densely populated regions of the country. Many people in Moscow live in high-rise apartment blocks.

MOVING EAST

Migration has been an important feature of Russia's population distribution for hundreds of years. One of the principal migratory patterns has been of people moving eastwards into Siberia from the more crowded central regions of European Russia. These European regions have a long history of settlement. People crossed the Ural Mountains into Siberia from the late sixteenth century onwards, as Russia sought to extend its boundaries. During the Soviet period (1917-91) this movement of peoples continued as the economic development of Siberia's natural resources became a priority. With the continuing development of Siberian energy and mineral resources, there remains an eastwards flow of people into Siberia.

Focus on: Emigration

Russia has experienced several waves of emigration over the last hundred years as people sought to flee the effects of revolution, war and the emergence of communism. The latter half of the twentieth century also witnessed a substantial religion-based emigration of Russian Jews to Israel, with an estimated 2 million leaving Russia (then the USSR) between 1945 and 1991.

Since the collapse of the USSR, emigration has been primarily for economic reasons with many educated and skilled Russians leaving in search of better paid jobs and a higher standard of living. Expatriate Russian communities are today particularly established in Europe, the USA and eastern Asia.

CHAPTER 5

Government and Politics

At the start of the twentieth century Russia was still ruled as an autocratic empire by a tsar (see pages 8-10) who took all key decisions and whose word was law. In 1905, however, dissatisfaction with this system triggered a process of radical political changes and Nicholas II was forced to concede some of his powers and establish the beginnings of a constitutional monarchy. A government and parliament, the Duma, was formed and granted powers to oversee the introduction of all new laws. In reality power remained with Nicholas, the last of Russia's tsars, who would simply close down the parliament if its members disagreed with him. By February 1917, however, mismanagement of the country had led to the forced abdication of Nicholas II in what became the first phase of the Russian Revolution.

COMMUNISM AND THE SOVIET UNION

The second phase of the Russian Revolution in October 1917 saw an alliance of workers' councils (soviets) seize control of the country from the weak provisional government. This marked the start of the communist era and, by 1922, the Union of Soviet Socialist Republics (USSR or Soviet Union) had been formed. In the Soviet Union, the Communist Party of the Soviet Union (CPSU) was the sole political party and its representatives controlled all aspects of government and decision making. Party members occupied positions of authority throughout all official institutions in the country.

Within the CPSU, the politburo (or principal policy-making committee) was the elite group

► Russian activists from left-wing organizations bear red flags as they march through central Moscow in September 2005 to protest against the 'capitalist' policies of the Russian government and president.

with, theoretically at least, the highest authority to take decisions. Also important were the central committee and the secretariat, which controlled party policy and administration. Despite these structures, the greatest power lay with the general secretary, particularly during the Stalin era when the Russian leader occupied the position as a virtual dictator from the mid-1920s until his death in 1953. After this, efforts were made to allocate power more widely, but the post of general secretary remained of major importance and status up until the collapse of the Soviet Union in 1991.

A NEW ERA

Since 1991 Russia has been governed as a federal republic, with a president as the chief of state. The president is elected by popular vote and serves a four-year term. The government itself is headed by a premier who is appointed by the president with the approval of the Duma (the pre-revolutionary name for the lower chamber of parliament). The premier also acts in place of a vice-president should the president become unfit for office, or die.

The Duma comprises 450 members who are elected every four years by popular vote. An upper chamber of parliament, the Federation Council, has 178 members appointed by the top legislative and executive officials in Russia's 89 federal administrative regions – each region appointing two members.

Did you know?

Women are poorly represented in Russian politics – for example, there are only 44 women members of the 450-member Duma. In the Federation Council representation is even lower; there are just 9 women among its 178 members.

▲ The deputies of Russia's Duma pose for a photograph following one of their state meetings.

The political division of Russia into 89 federal administrative units has changed little since Soviet times. Each unit is controlled by a governor appointed by the president. The governors have considerable powers, but must ensure that local policies conform to those of the president. The cities of Moscow and St Petersburg are independent of surrounding regions and are governed by elected mayors.

REFORM AND RESISTANCE

Russia's first democratically elected president was Boris Yeltsin in 1991, who remained in power until his resignation at the end of 1999. Yeltsin introduced radical political and economic reforms to modernize Russia, but these met with considerable resistance from the Congress of the People's Deputies, an assembly of representatives of local councils that had survived from Soviet times. In 1993 there was an attempted coup against Yeltsin in Moscow. However, the security service and army rallied to his cause and, using force, regained control of the parliament buildings. Opposition to Yeltsin was crushed in a ten-day conflict during which, according to the government, 187 people were killed and a further 437 were wounded, almost all of them anti-Yeltsin protesters. With his authority re-established, Yeltsin introduced a new constitution in 1993 and proceeded with far-reaching reforms to restructure and open up Russia's economy. Vladimir Putin, who succeeded Yeltsin as president, has continued with these reforms, but concerns have been expressed about the re-emergence of state intervention (see below) during his presidency.

Focus on: Presidential power

Despite political reforms, the Russian president retains substantial independent powers. The president can pass decrees without consent from parliament and is the head of both the armed forces and the national security council. The president also appoints all the main state officials, who are then able to exercise their powers throughout the Russian federation. Officially, the president is not affiliated to any political party, but Vladimir Putin enjoys strong support from the United Russia Party, which dominates contemporary politics. Some political commentators believe that the president has too much power in Russia. Under Vladimir Putin there has been an increase in state control of the economy, particularly in those sectors that are powerful, vast and lucrative, such as the energy sector (see pages 26-7).

▶ Boris Yeltsin (with paper in hand) delivers a speech while standing on top of an armoured vehicle outside the government building in Moscow. He was speaking out against the attempted coup that took place against Gorbachev in August 1991.

► Chechen protesters in Berlin, Germany, stand in front of a poster of Russian president Vladimir Putin to register their opposition towards his policy in Chechnya. The protest in February 2003 was timed to coincide with a two-day state visit to Germany by Putin.

Nevertheless, Putin was re-elected as president with 71 per cent of the vote in March 2004.

THE CHECHNYA PROBLEM

In November 1991 the republic of Chechnya declared itself independent of Russia under the leadership of Dzhokhar Dudayev, a former Soviet general. Russia refused to accept the secession and supported groups opposed to Dudayev in attempting to regain control of Chechnya. These attempts failed, and in December 1994 Russia sent in the military to reclaim Chechnya. There followed more than two years of war, until a ceasefire was agreed in May 1997. However, the ceasefire proved weak and fighting resumed in 1999. The conflict also spread, with Chechen terrorists carrying out bombings and hostage sieges elsewhere in Russia. Hundreds of people were killed in these actions and Russia launched anti-terrorism actions in Chechnya in an effort to

hunt down the killers. As some stability returned, a referendum was held in 2003 that gave Chechnya greater powers but kept it as part of the Russian federation. In 2004, however, the new pro-Russian president of Chechnya, Akhmad Kadyrov, was murdered in a bomb attack. In the same year, a siege by Chechen terrorists at a school in the Russian town of Beslan on the Chechen border led to the deaths of 331 people, half of them children. Fresh elections were held in 2005, but violence and opposition to Russia has spread beyond Chechnya into neighbouring provinces. The bringing of stability to this region is one of Russia's most significant political challenges.

? Did you know?

At least 100,000 people are believed to have died in the conflict in Chechnya and up to 500,000 people have been forced to flee their homes.

CHAPTER 6

Energy and Resources

Several decades ago, the Soviet Union and the USA were the world's two great superpowers. Today Russia has lost much of the political and military might it used to have as the Soviet Union, but it is re-emerging in the twenty-first century as a new type of superpower – an energy superpower.

NATURAL GAS

Russia has more proven natural gas reserves than any other country, accounting for 27 per cent of the global total in 2005. It is also the world's biggest producer (22 per cent of global total) and exporter (30 per cent of global exports) of natural gas, with a particularly dominant position in the European markets. For example, Germany, the world's third largest economy, depends on Russia for 41 per cent of its natural gas imports, while France and Italy obtain around a third of their gas imports from Russia. The significance of

Russian gas supplies became highly evident in January 2006, when a dispute with Ukraine over the price it paid for Russian gas led to the risk of European supplies (carried via a pipeline through Ukraine) being cut off. The dispute was resolved and gas flows were only slightly disrupted, but the incident made it very clear that many countries depend on Russian gas. This dependency is likely to increase as other sources run out and, by 2020, energy experts estimate that the European Union (EU) may depend on Russian gas to meet as much as 45 per cent of its total energy needs.

▼ A crane lifts up a segment of the Baltic Sea gas pipeline near the town of Babayevo in the Vologda region, some 650 km (400 miles) north-east of Moscow. The laying of this new pipeline was started by Gazprom (see box opposite) in December 2005. The pipeline will take Siberian gas directly to Germany across the floor of the Baltic Sea.

OIL

Russia has around 6 per cent of the world's known oil reserves and is the world's second biggest producer after Saudi Arabia, accounting for 12 per cent of global production in 2005. Production fell in the first years of post-Soviet Russia, but high world prices for oil have seen Russian production rise again to almost maximum levels. Over 70 per cent of Russia's crude oil is exported, and two-thirds of this goes to Europe where it is used primarily to heat European homes. Russia also refines oil and has around 40 oil refineries, but many of these are in need of modernization and repair because they were neglected during the Soviet period.

COAL

Russian coal reserves comprise around 17 per cent of the world total – only the USA has greater reserves. Like the oil industry though,

▶ The majority of Russia's oil reserves are located in Siberia. This oil derrick stands in the Vazeyskaya oil field.

Energy data

- Energy consumption as % of world total: 6.2%
- Energy consumption by sector (% of total):
  - Industry: 33.7
  - Transportation: 20.1
  - Agriculture: 3.5
  - Services: 6.3
  - Residential: 33.1
  - Other: 3.3
- CO_2 emissions as % of world total: 6.4
- CO_2 emissions per capita in tonnes p.a.: 10.16

Source: IEA

Focus on: Gazprom

The Russian gas industry is controlled by a part (38 per cent) state-owned monopoly called Gazprom that was established in 1993 to take over state gas production from the Soviet era. Gazprom produces nearly 90 per cent of Russia's gas, owns 60 per cent of known reserves and controls the pipelines for the distribution and export of Russian gas. Economically, Gazprom is responsible for around 8 per cent of Russia's GDP and 20 per cent of the federal budget. It also employs around 300,000 people in its direct and subsidiary operations.

coal was neglected during the last years of the Soviet era and this, combined with a falling global demand for coal during the 1990s, led to a slump in production from around 312 million tonnes (307 million tons) in 1992 to 214 million tonnes (211 million tons) by 1998. The coal industry has since been restructured and a growing demand for coal in Asia has seen production increase again to near 270 million tonnes (266 million tons) in 2004.

ELECTRICITY PRODUCTION

Russia not only produces large quantities of energy, it is also a major energy consumer – the third largest in the world. Electricity production in Russia comes primarily from its vast fossil fuel resources. Russian natural gas alone generates more than 44 per cent of electricity supplies. HEP facilities such as those on the Volga River (see page 16) contribute just over 17 per cent of Russia's electricity, and HEP

▼ A coal miner stands near industrial facilities in the Siberian city of Novokuznetsk, one of many mining and industrial cities that sprang up during Stalin's era.

is the main non-fossil fuel source of electricity. The other is nuclear power, which accounts for around 16 per cent of electricity production. Russia has 31 nuclear reactors, all of them in European Russia. Its safety record remains good, although 15 of its power stations have fewer than ten years remaining of their planned 30-year life and most are of the same design that failed so dramatically at Chernobyl (in Ukraine) in 1986. By 2010, the Russian Ministry

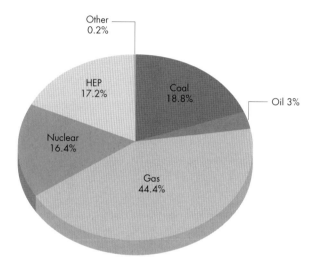

▲ Electricity production by type

► Nickel is smelted here in the Siberian city of Norilsk. Nickel is one of Russia's main non-energy mineral resources. Smelting nickel produces large quantities of toxic dust and pollution. Arctic winds carry pollution from Russian smelters like this as far as Canada and Scandinavia.

of Atomic Energy intends to build new production units at five of the existing sites and aims to have doubled nuclear electricity production by 2020.

NON-ENERGY RESOURCES

Russia has some of the world's largest deposits of minerals including iron and nickel ore, gold, diamonds and many non-ferrous metals and non-metallic minerals. However, many of these are difficult to extract because they are in remote areas with very hostile climates. Despite this, Russia is still a leading producer of various minerals, accounting in 2003 for 22 per cent of the world's nickel production, 16 per cent of its diamonds, and around 7 per cent of gold and iron ore production.

 Did you know?

The iron ore deposits of the Kursk Magnetic Anomaly, close to the Ukrainian border in the south-west of Russia, are believed to contain one-sixth of the world's total reserves.

Focus on: Russian forestry

About 22 per cent of the world's forests and 50 per cent of its coniferous forests are in Russia. They cover an area larger than the continental USA. Of Russia's 764 million hectares (1.88 billion acres) of forests, 78 per cent are in Siberia and the far east of the country. Only 55 per cent of the forested area is of commercial value and access is problematic because over half of Russian forests grow on permafrost soils unsuitable for road or rail. As a result, Russia presently accounts for only 3 per cent of the world's timber production and much of this is as lumber (rough sawn wood) rather than the more profitable processed timber.

CHAPTER 7

Economy and Income

In 2004 the Russian economy grew by around 7 per cent – faster than any of the world's other leading industrial powers. 2004 was also the sixth year in succession that the economy had grown, mainly as the result of high world oil prices and increasing global demand for Russian energy exports.

ENERGY DEPENDENCY

Russia's heavy dependence on energy exports means that its economy is especially vulnerable to changes in world oil prices. It has been estimated that a US$1 change in the price of a barrel of oil equates to a US$1.4 billion change in Russian revenues. Since the year 2000, high oil prices (brought about mainly by conflict and uncertainty in the oil-rich Gulf region of the Middle East) have afforded Russia record levels of oil earnings. In recognition of this windfall, in January 2004 the Russian government established a stabilization fund. This will enable Russia to store some of its oil profits to guard against any future downturn in the price of oil and therefore, the Russian economy. By the end of 2005 the stabilization fund was estimated to be worth around US$52 billion – equivalent to approximately 7 per cent of Russia's annual income in the same year. The government is under political pressure to spend some of this fund in order to improve immediate social conditions such as housing and healthcare, but financial experts warn that injecting so much money into these areas could lead to high inflation and damage to the economy.

KEEPING A BALANCE

Russia's so-called 'petrodollar boom' follows a decade of economic turmoil. During the Soviet era, virtually all aspects of the economy were centrally planned and controlled. Following the collapse of the Soviet Union, the planned economy was scrapped and Russia started to adopt a broadly free-market capitalist economy such as those of the USA, Japan and Europe.

◀ The headquarters of the energy company Gazprom in Moscow, the largest company in Russia. Gazprom produces around 8 per cent of national GDP. It is fast becoming one of the largest companies in the world.

Economic reforms had begun even before the end of the Soviet Union, but were too little and came too late. Industrial and agricultural output fell sharply in 1990-91. Russia's annual income in 1991 was more than 20 per cent lower than it had been in 1989 and the economy entered a five-year period of virtual collapse. People waited in long queues for supplies of even the most basic foodstuffs and industrial goods. By the mid-1990s there were signs of a recovery as private businesses and foreign investors began to buy in to the economy. People's standard of living improved, but the recovery was short-lived. A financial crisis that began in Asia in 1997 spread to Russia and led many investors to withdraw from the Russian economy. The government was forced to devalue the Russian currency to improve its competitiveness, but the economy and living standards had already deteriorated and, by 2000, the economy had shrunk to its 1960 levels. The petrodollar boom has since brought rapid economic growth, but analysts believe that a collapse in oil prices would be mirrored in the Russian economy and that Russia has yet to enter a period of secure economic growth.

▲ The TsUM shopping mall in Moscow has been extensively refurbished. It is one of the largest and most successful of the many retail centres in Russia.

Economic data

- Gross National Income (GNI) in US$: 639,080,000,000
- World rank by GNI: 15
- GNI per capita in US$: 4,460
- World rank by GNI per capita: 90
- Economic growth: 7.0%

Source: World Bank

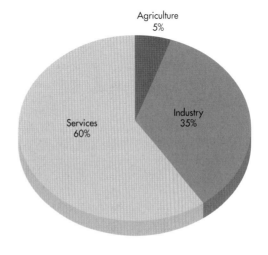

Agriculture
5%

Industry
35%

Services
60%

▲ Contribution by sector to national income

ECONOMIC STRUCTURE

Besides the energy and minerals sector, Russia's economy is based upon a balance of other industries (manufacturing and heavy industry), services and agriculture. The service sector (retail, banking, insurance, etc.) has expanded very quickly as Russia's internal market has developed and grown. Consumer demand, an important indicator of this growth, increased by over 12 per cent annually between 2000 and 2005. In 1989, services accounted for only 33 per cent of GDP, but by 2003 had increased to 60 per cent to become the largest sector of the economy.

The industrial sector dominated Russia under the Soviet Union and still accounted for 50 per cent of GDP in 1989, but by 2003 this had fallen to 35 per cent. A lack of investment during the Soviet era had left many industries inefficient and unable to compete in the new open, global market. Russia still has numerous large industries, however, particularly in metal fabrication, heavy engineering and chemicals.

▲ Despite the economic recovery and petrodollar windfalls, poverty remains a major problem in Russia. In January 2006 in Moscow, this elderly woman collects food from a distribution point for homeless people.

Agriculture as a proportion of GDP has fallen from 17 per cent of GDP in 1989 to just 5 per cent in 2003. Like industry, agriculture has suffered from years of under-investment and is still adjusting to the highly competitive global food markets. After considerable decline in the 1990s, favourable weather conditions during the period between 2001 and 2006 have resulted in

 Did you know?

In 1990, the US restaurant chain McDonald's became one of the first companies to take advantage of economic reforms when it opened a restaurant in Moscow. In 2006 it had 103 outlets in Russia, serving around 200,000 people per day.

a good recovery in yields of Russia's agricultural staples – wheat, barley and corn. Despite this, the poor state of farm machinery and continued restructuring of the entire farming sector mean that the contribution of agriculture to GDP is unlikely to increase in the foreseeable future.

Did you know?

In 1994 there were just four US$ billionaires in Russia. Today there are 36 – more than in the UK, France or Japan.

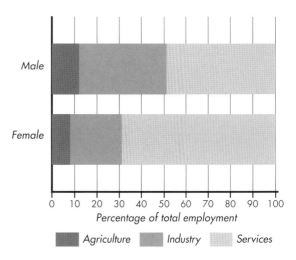

▲ Labour force by sector and gender

Focus on: Poverty and the new billionaires

Russia's economic transformation has caused considerable hardship for many ordinary Russian people. There is higher unemployment and greater poverty than there was at the end of the USSR era, and there are periodic shortages of supplies. In 2004, official government figures put the number of people living in poverty at around 25.5 million people, or 18 per cent of the population. Some individuals have benefited greatly, however, particularly those who purchased parts of the former Soviet energy

industry. Roman Abramovich is one such individual. In 2005 he was listed as the world's 21st wealthiest person (and the wealthiest Russian) with a personal fortune of US$13.3 billion. Besides oil, he has interests in politics and sport, owning a Russian hockey team and a leading UK soccer team, Chelsea Football Club. The new super-rich can assert considerable political influence and this has occasionally bought them into conflict with President Putin.

▶ Russian businessman Boris Berezovsky stands outside the Russian embassy in London, UK in 2004. He was protesting against the arrest for tax evasion of Russian billionaire, Mikhail Khodorkovsky, head of the Yukos oil company.

CHAPTER 8

Global Connections

Following the break-up of the Soviet Union, the new Russia was forced to come to terms with the fact that it was no longer one of the world's great superpowers. Today Russia is having to redefine its global relations and realign itself internationally.

THE COLD WAR ERA

In the aftermath of the Second World War, the Soviet Union and the USA emerged as the world's two great superpowers. However, these superpowers had very different political outlooks and considered each other a serious threat. The weapons of the Cold War were technological advancement, a display of military might, and political propaganda. There was an arms race to develop ever more destructive and far-reaching weapons, and a space race in which each side sought to outdo the other's latest technological achievements.

Although the USA and Soviet Union were never directly at war with each another, they engaged in numerous effective wars by supporting opposing regimes in other parts of the world by supplying them with weapons, funds and military support. The major wars in Korea (1950-53) and Vietnam (1954-75) are the clearest examples of this, but conflicts also raged elsewhere, such as in Afghanistan (1979-89).

MOVING FORWARD

The collapse of the Soviet Union in late 1991 signalled the end of the Cold War. Russia was the largest and most significant of the 15 countries to emerge from the Soviet Union and has been renegotiating its global relationships ever since. Russia's most important global connections are with Europe to the west, China to the east, Central Asia to the south and the important trading nations of the USA and Japan.

◀ The Russian military march at a Victory Day parade in May 2006. This event celebrates the historic Soviet victory in the Second World War. The Russian army is one of the world's largest active military forces.

The majority of Russia's people live in its western regions bordering Europe, which is also the focus for much of Russia's trade. The European Union in particular is a powerful and wealthy trading bloc. The EU expanded in 2004 to absorb the former Soviet countries of Estonia, Latvia and Lithuania. Bulgaria and Romania both have a history of strong political and economic ties with Russia (and before that, the Soviet Union); they joined the EU in 2007. These political shifts challenge Russia's influence in the region, but its large reserves of natural resources means that the EU is also heavily dependent on Russia.

▶ A photo from 1961 shows US soldiers with a tank near one of the checkpoints at the Berlin Wall – the most potent symbol of the Cold War era. A sign in English, Russian, French and German warns that: 'You are leaving the American sector' of Berlin.

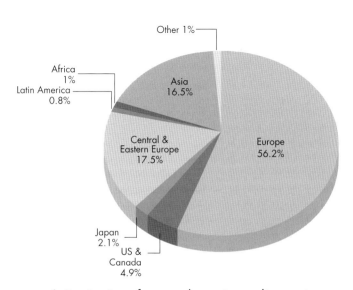

▲ Destination of exports by major trading region

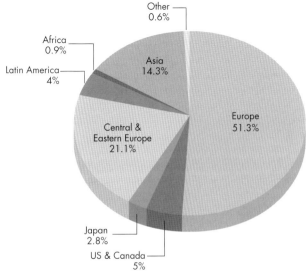

▲ Origin of imports by major trading region

To the east, Russia is geographically close to the fast-growing economies of China and South Korea and the more established Japanese economy. This region of Asia, and particularly China, is becoming an important centre of the global economy, challenging the strength of the EU and the USA. Russia is building strong relationships in this region, constructing oil pipelines from Siberia to supply China and Japan in return for greater Chinese and Japanese investment in the Russian economy. Russia's relationship with China is particularly significant. In 2001 the two countries signed the Treaty for Good Neighbourliness, Friendship and Co-operation as a symbol of their close ties. By August 2005, co-operation between Russia and China had been extended into defence, as their forces engaged in their first joint military exercises, known as Peace Mission 2005.

▼ Chinese marine vehicles landing in the China-Russia joint military exercise in August 2005. Peace Mission 2005 aimed to deepen mutual trust, promote friendship and enhance co-operation between the two nations.

Some political experts believe that the closer ties between Russia and China are a response to the dominant influence of the USA in world affairs. Russia, however, maintains that its relationship with the USA is just as important. The USA is a major trading partner for Russia and the two countries also co-operate in areas such as space exploration.

More recently, Russia and the USA have been united in the global fight against terrorism, following terrorist attacks on the USA in September 2001 and by Chechen separatists in Russia. The latter included a hostage siege at a Moscow theatre in 2002 and at a school in Beslan in 2004. Despite being united in their desire to defeat terrorism, Russia and the USA do not always agree on the actions to be taken. In 2003, for example, the USA and its allies (including the UK) invaded Iraq to overthrow the regime of its dictator, Saddam Hussein. They claimed that Saddam's government was supporting terrorist activity. Russia joined with France and Germany to criticize the action and argue for a diplomatic solution.

WORLD INFLUENCE

Russia occupies an influential role in global politics because of its inherited position as one of only five permanent members of the UN Security Council (the others are China, France, UK and USA), the body responsible for overseeing global peace and security. In 1998, Russia gained further global stature when it joined the G7 group of leading industrialized economies (to form the new G8). The G8 group meets annually to discuss global issues of mutual interest such as trade, poverty and security. In 2006, Russia held the presidency of the G8 for the first time, and the annual summit took place in St Petersburg.

▲ One of the major peace missions for Russian forces in recent years was their deployment in Kosovo as part of a NATO force. This soldier is part of a security escort for Serb children on their way to school in December 1999.

 Did you know?

During the Cold War era, the Soviet army was the largest active army in the world with between 3 and 5 million soldiers.

 Did you know?

In the 1992 Olympic Games, athletes belonging to countries of the CIS (see below) competed as a single unified team. They have since competed internationally as individual states.

Focus on: The Commonwealth of Independent States

The Commonwealth of Independent States (CIS) was created in December 1991 out of the break-up of the Soviet Union. It is an alliance (similar to the European Union) of 11 of the 15 former Soviet republics – Armenia, Azerbaijan, Belarus, Georgia, Kazakhstan, Kyrgyzstan, Moldova, Russia, Tajikistan, Ukraine and Uzbekistan. Turkmenistan is an associate member, having withdrawn from permanent membership in 2005. The CIS member countries co-operate on issues such as economics, security and foreign policy and, in particular, aim to establish a similar free trade zone as that of the European Union. Since 2003, political changes have seen several of the CIS member countries align themselves more closely with Europe and less closely with the CIS and Russia, its dominant nation. Some political experts question whether the CIS will continue to exist. However, all agree that Russia, as its largest and most politically important country, will play a vital role in determining the future of the CIS.

CHAPTER 9

Transport and Communications

Transport and communications are vital to a country of Russia's size, and were well established during the Soviet era. Following the break-up of the Soviet Union, Russia inherited much of its huge transport and communications network. Since then, Russia has undertaken a considerable amount of reorganization to create new systems that meet its present needs.

RAILWAYS

With 87,157 km (54,158 miles) of track, Russia's rail network is second only to the USA's in terms of its length. It is well connected to the 15 republics of the former Soviet Union because it was once part of the much larger Soviet rail network. In 1998 the government began to reform the network in a process that led, in September 2003, to the formation of a new public corporation, Russian Railways (RZD). The new structure opened up possibilities for greater investment in the railways, for example it allowed private operators to run trains on the existing network. It is still too early to assess the full impact of the reforms, but the Russian rail system remains vital to the economy.

AIR TRAVEL

Russia's vast size means that for many years it has made use of aviation as a means of transport, with a national airline that was founded under the Soviets as long ago as 1923. In 1932 this airline was named Aeroflot and

▼ A platform full of passengers greets a train on the Trans-Siberian Railway, one of the longest rail routes in the world that takes seven days to complete!

104

went on to become a pioneer in civil aviation, establishing the world's first passenger jet services in 1956. Following the collapse of the Soviet Union, Aeroflot was split into various national airlines to serve the newly independent states. The name Aeroflot was kept and used by the new Russian national air carrier. Aeroflot flies regular routes to 89 cities in 47 countries and has partnerships with other international airlines to further extend their services. Of the 89 cities served by Aeroflot, 25 of them are within Russia, which makes it the main domestic carrier, too.

Did you know?

Russia's railways carry more freight than any other railway in the world, except for China and the USA. Passenger movements are also significant, and in these Russia ranks fourth in the world, behind China, India and Japan.

▲ Passengers disembark from an Aeroflot aircraft at Riga International Airport in Latvia. Many of the national carrier's busiest air routes are within Russia or connect Russia to former Soviet republics such as Latvia.

Transport & communications data

- Total roads: 537,289 km/333,865 miles
- Total paved roads: 362,133 km/225,025 miles
- Total unpaved roads: 175,156 km/108,840 miles
- Total railways: 87,157 km/54,158 miles
- Airports: 1,623
- Cars per 1,000 people: 140
- Mobile phones per 1,000 people: 517
- Personal computers per 1,000 people: 132
- Internet users per 1,000 people: 111

Source: World Bank and CIA World Factbook

WATERWAYS

Russia's navigable waterways cover some 96,000 km (59,650 miles) and are second only to China's in their extent. They provide an important transport route for the import and export of freight as well as for movements within Russia. The most important waterways are a system of around 72,000 km (44,700 miles) in European Russia which connects the Baltic Sea, White Sea, Caspian Sea, Sea of Azov and Black Sea. In 2002 Russia signed an agreement to become part of a growing European inland waterway network that extends from the Atlantic Ocean in the west to the Ural Mountains in the east. It connects 37 countries and incorporates some 350 major ports.

MEDIA AND TELECOMMUNICATIONS

During the Soviet era, telecommunications and the media were heavily controlled by the state. Post-Soviet Russia has seen this change radically, with a greater freedom in the media (television, radio and press) and a proliferation of new communications technology such as mobile phones, email and the Internet.

The transition to an open and free media has not been smooth, however, and the Russian government has actually increased its control of the major media channels in recent times. For example, in 2002 the general manager of the NTV channel was fired for its coverage of the Moscow theatre siege because the channel's method of reporting angered President Putin. In 2005, a new satellite news channel, Russia Today, was launched as an English language channel to report global affairs from a Russian perspective. This too is funded and controlled by the government.

During the Soviet era, Russia's fixed-line telephone network was largely confined to the needs of the state and the military. Following the collapse of the Soviet Union it was anticipated that the industry would grow

◀ A cargo vessel on the Volga River near St Petersburg; the Volga is one of the most important of Russia's navigable waterways in terms of trade and transport.

Focus on: The Russian underground

During the Soviet era, the government declared that any city of more than a million people should have an underground rail system, or metro. As a result, six Russian cities have metro systems, with a further six planned or under construction. In 2005, the overall length of functioning metro lines was 420 km (261 miles), with 267 stations and an annual passenger capacity of more than 4 billion passengers. Tickets are inexpensive and trains are frequent and efficient. The most famous of the Russian underground rail systems is in Moscow. The first 12-km (7.5-mile) line was opened in 1935, and the metro has since expanded to 12 lines, 165 stations and more than 270 km (168 miles) of track. It is the world's busiest metro, carrying between 8 and 9 million passengers every weekday, with trains arriving every 90 seconds during peak hours.

▶ Commuters pass through one of the ornately decorated tunnels at Arbatskaya station on the Arbatsko-Pokrovskaya line of the Moscow metro.

rapidly. In reality, growth has been much slower because of the high subscriber costs involved and the emergence of mobile networks as an alternative. By 2005, only around 30 per cent of the population were connected to the fixed telephone network. In contrast, the mobile network has grown rapidly and by 2005 it was estimated to have reached 52 per cent of the population, up from just 5 per cent in 2001. Internet use has also grown rapidly in Russia, with around 13 per cent of the population having Internet access by 2005, an increase from only 3 per cent in 2001.

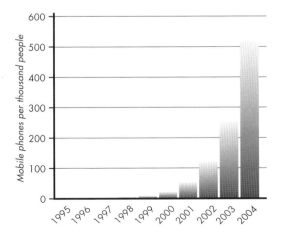

▲ Mobile phone use, 1995-2004

CHAPTER 10

Education and Health

Under Soviet control, education and healthcare were wholly funded by the state and available to all. The education system was rigid and standardized, but it was of a high quality and it helped the Soviet Union become a world leader in science and technology. Healthcare was also of a high standard, with one of the best patient-to-doctor ratios in the world. Russia inherited these systems, but has found them difficult to maintain.

EDUCATION

There is a high value placed on education in Russia, and discipline and attendance are good. Most students remain within the state funded education system, but private schools and specialist foreign language and international schools are now available for those able to afford them. Curriculum and examination procedures are being reviewed and the Soviet style of rote teaching is being replaced by approaches that encourage problem-solving and creative thinking. An example of these reforms is the introduction of greater specialization for 16 to 18 year olds. Under new proposals, senior pupils will specialize in just four or five subjects rather than the 12 or even 14 currently studied.

Education and health

- Life expectancy at birth, male: 58.8
- Life expectancy at birth, female: 72
- Infant mortality rate per 1,000: 16
- Under five mortality rate per 1,000: 21
- Physicians per 1,000 people: 4.3
- Health expenditure as % of GDP: 5.6%
- Education expenditure as % of GDP: 3.7%
- Primary net enrolment: 93%
- Pupil-teacher ratio, primary: 16.6
- Adult literacy as % age 15+: 99.4

Source: United Nations Agencies and World Bank

◀ Children play outside their school in the village of Bol'shoye Goloustnoye in Siberia, close to Lake Baikal. Recruiting teachers to work for any length of time in such remote locations is just one of the challenges facing Russia's education system.

▲ Schools equipped with new technology can offer a high quality education equivalent to that in Europe or the USA, but the provision of such facilities to all Russian schools is a hugely expensive undertaking.

Reform is not easy, however, with more than 63,000 schools and many staff who were themselves educated and trained under the former Soviet system. Recruiting new teachers into state schools is also problematic, as salaries are relatively low. English and IT teachers, for example, can earn higher incomes working for foreign-language schools or in business. The government is trying to address the problem with large increases in teachers' salaries.

HEALTHCARE
Russia has not been able to maintain the high standards of its healthcare system in a post-Soviet era and the health of its population has suffered as a result. For example, life expectancy at birth fell from 68 years in 1991 to 65.4 years in 2003 (compared with 77 years in

the USA and 78 years in the UK). Not all trends are negative, however, and some basic healthcare indicators have improved since 1991. Child immunization rates have increased from around 77 per cent of the population to 97 per cent, and infant mortality (the number of children dying before the age of one year) fell from 21 per 1,000 live births in 1991 to 16 per 1,000 live births by 2003.

UNDER PRESSURE
Of great concern is the increase in illnesses and deaths related to lifestyle habits, such as drinking and smoking. Alcoholism, especially among men, is a particular problem and it is causing higher levels of death by injury and an increase in the number of conditions such as heart and liver disease. Russia has among the highest number of smokers in the world, with 36 per cent of all adults in 2005 (62 per cent of adult men). The incidence of smoking has increased rapidly among women (particularly young, urban women) in recent years, from 10

Focus on: Higher education

During the Soviet era, higher education was state funded and students were paid a small state grant during their studies. They were also guaranteed a job upon graduation, though this was centrally allocated and could be very distant from their home town. Higher education is still state funded and desirable for many young people. Competition for places is intense and, as a result, some universities now supplement their state-funded places with additional fee-paying places. There are 48 universities in Russia and more than 500 higher education institutions (some of them private) with a total of some 3 million students between them.

▲ Students at Moscow State University, one of the most prestigious higher education institutes in the country.

per cent of adult women in 1994 to 15 per cent by 2005.

A rise in the incidence of diseases related to social habits, such as smoking and drinking alcohol, is placing additional pressure on an

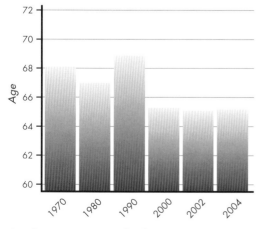

▲ Life expectancy at birth, 1970-2004

already overstretched health service. Many health facilities are in need of substantial modernization, and staff shortages are growing as a result of poor pay and working conditions. In addition, large variations are emerging in healthcare quality between the regions. In response to these changes, private healthcare is expanding rapidly and attracting many medical professionals away from the state system by offering higher pay and better opportunities.

Since the collapse of the Soviet Union, Russia has seen the start of an HIV/AIDS epidemic that experts fear could quickly spread out of control if urgent action is not taken. By the end of 2004 there were 300,000 officially registered cases of HIV, but under-reporting means that the real level is estimated to be as high as 1.4 million people living with HIV. The majority

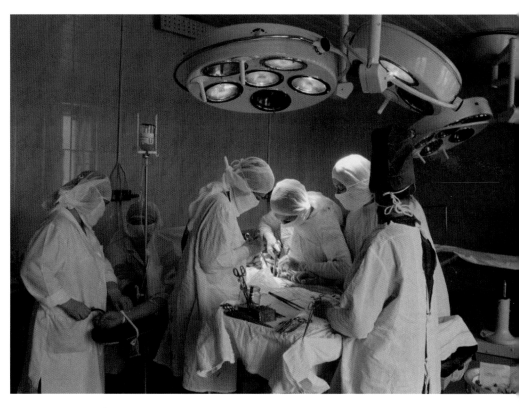

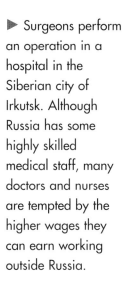

► Surgeons perform an operation in a hospital in the Siberian city of Irkutsk. Although Russia has some highly skilled medical staff, many doctors and nurses are tempted by the higher wages they can earn working outside Russia.

(around 80 per cent) of HIV cases are related to drug abuse and the use of infected needles. Sexual transmission (increasingly through prostitution) accounts for the balance of cases. HIV incidence is particularly high among Russia's youth (15-29 year olds) who account for three-quarters of reported new cases. The government seems unable to cope with the scale of the problem, providing only 10 per cent of patients with the necessary anti-retroviral drugs to delay the onset of AIDS. Needle exchange services and public education programmes are both being extended to try to halt the epidemic, but many experts believe it will get much worse before it gets better.

Focus on: TB and AIDS

Russia has one of the highest rates of tuberculosis (TB) in the world, with more than 121,000 new cases being identified in 2004. TB is particularly widespread among the prison population, but it is also prevalent in the population at large. The poor availability of drugs, together with increasingly drug-resistant forms of TB, has prolonged and extended the spread of TB to almost epidemic proportions. Russia is now engaged in a global strategy to combat the further spread of the disease through a World Health Organization programme.

Did you know?

In 2002, Russia's production and consumption of cigarettes was equivalent to 117 packets a year (or six cigarettes per day) for every single person. 270,000 people die of smoking related diseases each year in Russia, more than from AIDS, road accidents, drug abuse, murder and suicide put together.

CHAPTER 11

Culture and Religion

Russian culture and religion are heavily influenced by the political transitions of the country's history. During the Soviet era, for example, the communist government demanded that all art must serve the interests of the state and the Communist Party, and religion was suppressed in favour of a state policy of atheism. Today, culture and religion in Russia enjoy much greater freedoms, and a higher degree of external influence, too.

PRE-SOVIET CULTURE

Before the founding of the communist state, during the nineteenth and early part of the twentieth century, there was an era in which many of Russia's most famous cultural contributors were producing their works. They included the poet and writer, Alexander Pushkin (1799-1837), whose poetry continues to be popular with many Russians today.

In the mid-nineteenth century, the novels of Lev Nikolaevich Tolstoy (1828-1910), which included *War and Peace* (1869) and *Anna Karenina* (1877), made a significant contribution to Russian literature. Another important writer during this period was Fyodor Dostoevsky (1821-81) whose works included *Crime and Punishment* (1866), *The Idiot* (1869) and *The Brothers Karamazov* (1869). Tolstoy and Dostoevsky are widely recognized as being among the world's literary greats. Another famous Russian writer is the dramatist, Anton Chekhov (1860-1904), who although best known for his plays such as *The Three Sisters* (1901) and *The Cherry Orchard* (1904), also wrote many short stories.

Several of Russia's most famous composers were also active during the pre-communist era. They included Nikolay Rimsky-Korsakov (1844-1908) and Alexander Borodin (1833-87) who were known for their operatic works, but who also

◀ Dmitri Gudanov, a dancer with the Bolshoi Ballet, performs in *Swan Lake* at the Royal Opera House in London, UK in August 2006. The Bolshoi is Russia's most famous ballet and a major touring production company.

Focus on: Alexander Solzhenitsyn

One of the best known writers to have been sanctioned during the Soviet era is Alexander Solzhenitsyn (1918-). Solzhenitsyn first fell foul of the Soviet regime when he wrote a letter criticizing Stalin shortly after the Second World War. He was sentenced to eight years in prison and labour camps. This harsh experience became the basis for Solzhenitsyn's first published work *One Day in the Life of Ivan Denisovich* (1962), which was initially well received by a post-Stalin USSR. As his writing became openly critical of the government of the day, however, he found his works banned and resorted to publishing abroad or to *samizdat* (illegal self-publishing). Solzhenitsyn was awarded the Nobel Prize for Literature in 1970, but was unable to collect it for fear of not being allowed to return to the USSR. Three years later, in 1973, his book *The Gulag Archipelago* looked at the extensive Russian prison system and it led to Solzhenitsyn being arrested for treason. He was deported in February 1974. It was not until *glasnost* became a new Soviet policy in the late 1980s that Solzhenitsyn's work was published again in the USSR. In 1990, his Soviet citizenship was restored, and he eventually returned to Russia in 1994.

▶ Alexander Solzhenitsyn enjoys a walk shortly after his return to Russia in 1994.

wrote a wide range of music based on traditional Russian themes. The most significant composer of this time, however, was Pyotr Tchaikovsky (1840-93), who became the first Russian composer to attract major attention from outside his home country. Some of his most famous works include the opera *Eugene Onegin* (1879), the ballet *The Nutcracker* (1892) and grand orchestral pieces such as *Romeo and Juliet* (1870).

Under the Soviets, many of the literary and musical traditions of pre-communist Russia continued, but a large number of artists and writers felt the need to emigrate in order to have creative freedom. Under Stalin's 'Socialist Realism' policies, all art forms were required to serve the interests of the USSR. Much of the cultural output during this period was mundane and of limited interest, but there were exceptions. In literature, authors such as Boris Pasternak (1890-1960) and Alexander Solzhenitsyn (1918-) continued to produce strong novels, while in classical music, Dmitry Shostakovich (1906-75) and Sergei Rachmaninov (1873-1943) made significant contributions.

POST-SOVIET CULTURE

Since the political transformations of 1991, Russians have become very interested in re-examining their pre-Soviet culture and elements of the Soviet era itself. This interest is motivated by a desire to regain aspects of Russia's cultural heritage. Russian artists and writers, such as Alexander Solzhenitsyn (see previous page), whose works were shunned or even banned during the Soviet era, are now finding new audiences and recognition. There is also a wealth of new influences as Russia's culture, like all other aspects of life, is affected by the opening up of Russia to wider global forces. Film, music, art and literature from outside Russia bring new experiences, not just for audiences but for Russian artists too, who now enjoy complete artistic freedom, limited only by what consumers will buy.

RELIGION

Since Russia was converted in 988, the official state religion has been Orthodox Christianity. In the fifteenth century, the Russian Orthodox Church emerged as a form of orthodoxy that was distinct from the broader Eastern Orthodox Church. The Soviet era ushered in changes as the Church was separated from the state and the Soviet Union became officially atheist. The communist government (particularly under Stalin) tried to suppress religion in the belief that it was incompatible with the ideals of the Communist Party. Possessions from the Orthodox Church were seized and many churches and cathedrals were destroyed.

In 1985 this suppression of religion was relaxed and, in 1990, new laws guaranteeing religious freedom came into force. Christianity, and specifically Orthodox Christianity, remains the largest religion in Russia today, though several other forms of Christianity are now becoming popular. Russia's other main religions are Islam and Judaism. Many Russian Jews emigrated to Israel following the end of the Soviet era and the subsequent removal of travel restrictions. Today Jews in Russia make up a small minority (about 0.4 per cent) of the population. Islam is more prevalent, accounting for almost 8 per

◀ During Christmas ceremonies, Russian girls light candles in a church in the village of Zhilino, some 20 km (12.5 miles) outside Moscow. The Russian Orthodox Church celebrates Christmas on 7 January.

cent of the population, but it is heavily concentrated in central and southern regions of the country. Some Islamist factions have been linked to the troubled south of Russia, where there is an ongoing struggle by some regions (particularly Chechnya) for independence from Moscow. Islamic militant groups have been blamed for numerous acts of terrorism against Russian civilians and accused of having links with wider organizations, such as al-Qaeda.

▲ The Great Mosque in the city of Kazan was destroyed by Ivan the Terrible, but was rebuilt in 1996 with the aid of funds from Saudi Arabia. It is the largest mosque in Russia.

? Did you know?

Before the Russian Revolution, there were 54,000 functioning parishes and more than 150 bishops in Russia. By 1939, there were fewer than 100 functioning parishes and only four bishops. Today, the Church has more than 23,000 parishes and 154 bishops.

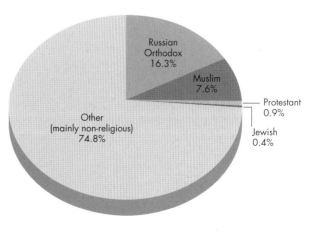

Russian Orthodox 16.3%

Muslim 7.6%

Protestant 0.9%

Jewish 0.4%

Other (mainly non-religious) 74.8%

▲ Major religions

CHAPTER 12

Leisure and Tourism

During the Soviet era, leisure was a state-sponsored activity. Sports facilities, theatres, cinemas, galleries and museums were all subsidized by the state, providing universal access for little or no payment. Tourism within the country was very under-developed, although the number of resorts, sanatoria, hotels and other tourist facilities grew gradually over time. A special passport was needed for foreign trips and this was only issued to the most privileged members of the Communist Party. In post-Soviet Russia, the situation is dramatically different.

RUSSIAN TOURISTS ABROAD

Restrictions on foreign travel were relaxed soon after the collapse of the Soviet Union. Since then, rising living standards have enabled many Russians to take holidays abroad. Among the most popular countries visited by Russians are Turkey, France, Germany, Egypt and Poland, all of which allow free (non-visa) passage for Russian passport holders. President Putin is working with other European countries to remove visa requirements and encourage greater travel between Russia and Europe. Beyond Europe, Asian destinations such as Vietnam and Thailand are increasingly popular with Russians.

TOURISM IN RUSSIA

The number of foreign tourists visiting Russia grew dramatically in the years following the end of the Soviet era. By 1995, numbers had reached 10 million visitors per year and they peaked at just short of 23.2 million in 2002. Since then, the number of tourists has reduced considerably to around 22.2 million visitors in 2003 and 2004. A quarter of all visitors to Russia head for Moscow, drawn by the city's

◀ Tourists stroll in the plaza in front of the Winter Palace in St Petersburg. Built between 1754 and 1762, it was once home to the tsars of Imperial Russia, but is now best known as part of the world famous Hermitage museum.

numerous attractions, which include Red
Square, the Kremlin buildings and Lenin's
mausoleum. St Petersburg is another favourite
destination, famous for its impressive
architecture and its cultural attractions. These
include the Hermitage museum that, with more
than three million items, houses one of the
largest and most important art collections in the
world. Beyond the appeal of the so-called 'twin
capitals' of Moscow and St Petersburg, tourists
flock to the coastal resorts around the Black Sea
and, in winter, to the ski resorts in the Caucasus
and Ural mountains.

With tourism set to become the world's biggest
industry during the twenty-first century, Russia
is keen to share in the potential benefits. There
are many possibilities for tourist activities and
Russian entrepreneurs have been quick to
exploit outside interest. The most extreme
example of this is space tourism! Foreign
nationals are willing to pay US$20 million and
train for months for the chance to become one

▲ Winter sports enthusiasts enjoy skiing on Mount
Cheget in the Caucasus Mountains, one of Russia's
main ski resorts.

of the growing number of 'space tourists' who
have travelled to the International Space Station
on a Russian rocket. In 2001, Denis Tito from
the USA became the first space tourist and, by
2007, three others had followed him. Tourist
places on planned Russian missions are now
fully booked until 2009.

SPORT

During the Soviet period the Communist Party
considered success in sports at a global level as
proof of its superiority. Football (soccer) is the
most popular sport in Russia and draws
considerable support. In the 2004-5 season, CSKA
Moskva (Moscow) won one of Europe's most
prestigious football competitions, the UEFA
(Union of European Football Associations) Cup.
CSKA was the first Russian side to do so. Other

popular sports include track and field athletics, gymnastics and tennis, and Russia has achieved considerable international success in all of these. In tennis in particular Russia has produced a number of young stars, including Yevgeny Kafelnikov and Nikolay Davydenko in the men's game and Anna Kournikova and Maria Sharapova, the winner of the 2004 Wimbledon title, in women's tennis.

Russia's climate means that winter sports are also popular and Russia (previously as the USSR) has long been one of the world's dominant nations in figure skating and ice hockey. In recent times, however, this dominance has been reduced. It has been suggested that reasons for this are a reduction in the level of spending on sport by the government and the closure of many sporting facilities. The result has been that there is less opportunity for people, particularly the young, to participate in sports. Many private health and leisure facilities have opened to meet the needs of Russia's growing middle classes, but such places are expensive and beyond the reach of most Russians. In 2005, the government announced new spending plans for a programme of more

than 4,000 new sports facilities, to be built between 2006 and 2015. President Putin said the aim was to make sports facilities and healthy living available to as many people as possible. Over half of the new facilities are to be targeted at children and young people, and with this in mind they are being built alongside schools or higher education institutions.

Did you know?

In the March 2006 world tennis rankings there were six Russian women in the top twenty – more than from any other country, and twice the number of the next best country, France.

LEISURE

Modern Russians enjoy the same broad range of leisure activities as people in any country in the developed world. Western popular culture used to be banned in the USSR, but people are now free to have the same interests, watch the same films and listen to the same music as their counterparts in the West. The Internet is increasingly popular and accessible in Russia. There are many talented and innovative

◀ The frozen surface of the Angara River in Irkutsk provides a group of boys with the chance for an informal game of ice hockey. Russia is among the world's most successful nations in this fast-moving winter sport.

Russians working in IT, and enabling the country to make rapid progress in catching up after the years of Soviet isolation.

Focus on: The *dacha*

A specifically Russian way of spending leisure time is to visit the *dacha*. A *dacha* is a vacation or summer house that many Russian families have in addition to their urban apartment. The *dacha* is always in the countryside, often near a lake or river, and can be anything from a modest wooden hut to an elaborate, brick-built house with sauna, satellite dish and full central heating. Russians love to escape the bustle of city life, usually in the summer but sometimes all year round, to retreat for the weekend or longer to the clean air and the quiet of the country.

▲ A group of older men play chess on a park bench along Nevsky Prospekt, one of the main thoroughfares in St Petersburg.

Tourism in Russia

- Tourist arrivals, millions: 22.051
- Earnings from tourism in US$: 6,958,000,000
- Tourism as % foreign earnings: 3.4
- Tourist departures, millions: 24.410
- Expenditure on tourism in US$: 16,527,000,000

Source: World Bank

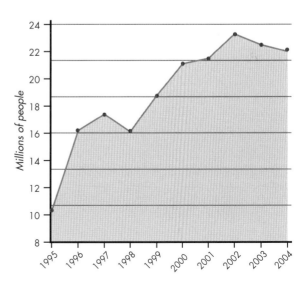

▲ Changes in international tourism, 1995-2004

CHAPTER 13

Environment and Conservation

With such a vast landscape, there are parts of Russia that are virtually untouched by human activity. Despite this, the Russian environment is sometimes far from healthy and faces numerous challenges, many of them associated with years of neglect during the Soviet administration.

THE SOVIET LEGACY

The policies of the Soviet era focused on rapid industrialization and economic growth, at almost any cost. For over half a century, these policies saw industrial, mining and nuclear wastes, agricultural chemicals and human wastes (raw sewage) discharged, unmonitored, into Russia's rivers and lakes. There was a similar disregard for air quality, and atmospheric pollution from the industrial, energy, transport and domestic sectors was among the highest in the world. Studies completed in the late 1990s found that more than 200 Russian cities failed to meet nationally accepted guidelines (similar to guidelines used in the USA and elsewhere). In eight cities (those associated with heavy industry in particular), air quality was up to ten times worse than accepted Russian health standards recommended.

The economic downturn that followed the collapse of the Soviet Union saw many of Russia's industries reduce production or close altogether. This gave the Russian environment some short-term relief from pollutants and allowed some degree of recovery. The opening up of the economy, the desire for rapid economic growth and higher personal incomes all brought new pressures, however. These included the rapid increase in car ownership which results in more atmospheric pollution. In 1991, Russia had roughly 87 vehicles for every 1,000 people, but by 2001 this had more than doubled to 176 vehicles per 1,000 people. Along with increased levels of consumption and the expansion of Russia's

◀ A heavily polluted forest near the Kolva River in the Usinsk region. This area has been contaminated by oil leaking into streams from corroded pipelines. Many of Russia's industries have poor environmental standards.

mining and energy sectors, these new sources of pollution threaten to halt any decrease resulting from industrial decline.

GROWING AWARENESS

Environmental awareness is growing in Russia, and the government recognizes that it can no longer ignore the environmental impacts of its policies. The cost of cleaning up decades of neglect is high, however, and so many demands for funding mean that Russia's environmental budget is limited. Nevertheless Russia has signalled its willingness to address the issues seriously. In November 2004, for example, Russia ratified the 1997 Kyoto Protocol to reduce emissions of greenhouse gases by at least 5 per cent of their 1990 levels by 2012. While the USA refuses to ratify the Kyoto Protocol, Russia's involvement, as the world's third biggest contributor of carbon dioxide (the main greenhouse gas), is vital. Russia should easily meet its Kyoto commitments: some estimate that Russian emissions may be 20 per cent below their 1990 levels already. Under a complex carbon trading agreement, Russia

could earn millions of dollars by selling its surplus allowances to those countries that are finding it harder to meet their commitments.

▲ Firemen spray special foam to neutralize oil spills on the surface of the Baltic Sea during a 2004 training exercise near the town of Baltiisk in the Kaliningrad region. The exercise was to test responses to a mass casualty and environmental disaster situation caused by a terrorist attack.

 Did you know?

The Russian government has estimated that poor air quality is a contributing factor to 17 per cent of child illnesses and 10 per cent of adult illnesses in the country.

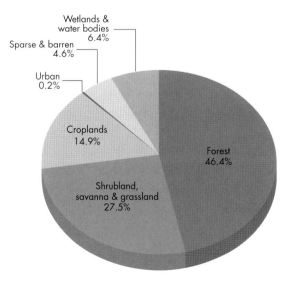

Wetlands &
water bodies
6.4%

Sparse & barren
4.6%

Urban
0.2%

Croplands
14.9%

Forest
46.4%

Shrubland,
savanna & grassland
27.5%

▲ Habitat type as a percentage of total area

POPULAR PRESSURE

Today Russian people have greater access to information about the environment. They can now find out about worldwide environmental pressure movements such as Greenpeace and Friends of the Earth. Greenpeace began operating in Russia in 1989 and has carried out campaigns on various issues, including the protection of fragile habitats (such as Lake Baikal, see box opposite), deforestation and replanting initiatives, and the safety and regulation of Russia's nuclear industry.

THE NUCLEAR CHALLENGE

One of the biggest threats to Russia's environment is from nuclear waste. Many of Russia's nuclear power stations are nearing the end of their operational life and will need to be decommissioned (shut down) in a process that generates vast amounts of highly radioactive waste. In addition to dealing with its own nuclear waste, Russia has also agreed to treat and store nuclear waste from other countries. The government believes it can do this safely, and that by specializing in the handling of nuclear waste it can also earn valuable foreign revenue. Campaign groups such as Greenpeace are less convinced and fear another nuclear accident such as the one that occurred at Chernobyl in 1986 and led to radioactive material being spread across a large part of northern Europe.

Environmental and conservation data

📁 Forested area as % total land area: 46.4

📁 Protected area as % total land area: 11.2

📁 Number of protected areas: 664

SPECIES DIVERSITY

Category	Known species	Threatened species
Mammals	90	14
Breeding birds	250	5
Reptiles	55	4
Amphibians	44	4
Fish	168	9
Plants	5,599	3

Source: World Resources Institute

◀ A Ukrainian woman lights a candle in memory of firemen who died fighting the disaster at the Chernobyl nuclear power plant in 1986. The Chernobyl disaster still casts a shadow over Russia's nuclear policies.

Another potential source of nuclear pollution comes from the decommissioning of naval submarines that were dumped off the north coast of Russia during the Soviet era. There is real concern that over time, these submarines could leak radioactive materials into the northern seas and in doing so contaminate fish and other aquatic life.

Did you know?

Russia has two unique species of large cat, the Amur tiger and the Amur leopard, and both are highly endangered. There are fewer than 40 Amur leopards left in the wild, and Amur tigers, the largest cats in the world, are thought to number fewer than 500.

▶ Crew members wait on board the new Gepard super-silent nuclear submarine. Nuclear energy remains important to Russia's naval fleet, despite a series of accidents involving nuclear submarines and concerns over their safety.

Focus on: Lake Baikal

Baikal is the deepest lake on earth. It has 365 rivers flowing into it and only one river flowing out of it. Approximately half of the 2,615 plant and animal species found in the Baikal region are unique to the lake and its immediate surroundings. There are more than 560 species of algae in Baikal and 52 species of fish. The omul (an Arctic white fish that can only be found in Baikal) accounts for two-thirds of the annual catch from the lake.

The most unique animal at Baikal is the freshwater seal known as the nerpa, which is also the only mammal to inhabit the lake. Scientists are unsure as to how a seal has ended up in the middle of Asia when other members of its species all live in polar regions to the north. The favoured theory is that the nerpa seals arrived in Lake Baikal during the last ice age when advancing polar ice pushed southwards.

There are currently estimated to be 60,000 nerpa in Lake Baikal. Their population faces threats from hunting (around 3,500 young nerpa are killed each year for their skins) and from increased levels of pollutants in the water. One of the main sources of pollution is the Baikalsk pulp and paper plant, which has been pumping chlorine and other chemicals into the lake since 1966.

CHAPTER 14

Future Challenges

Looking ahead, the entire future of Russia remains a considerable challenge. It is a vast landmass to govern politically, especially when there are very real divides on the basis of ethnicity, religion and wellbeing (quality of life). President Putin has introduced stringent reforms in an attempt to bring about a rapid improvement of Russia's economy and general living conditions, but many of his policies have encountered considerable criticism. There is concern that too much power has been regained by the state and that the president in particular has excessive power. For example, several media networks have been closed down or nationalized, and many people say this has happened because the networks spoke out against Putin and the Russian government.

The legacy of the Soviet era also remains apparent in many aspects of Russian life, for example in the poor state of the environment. Air, water and soil pollution are, in places, among the worst in the world and there is an urgent need to improve the regulation of future economic growth so that Russia's natural habitats are not further damaged. Healthcare and education are also in need of considerable attention to reverse the negative health trends that characterized Russia's early post-Soviet era.

▼ An old woman begs for money from passers-by on a cold street in Moscow. Resolving the enormous inequalities in wealth that have emerged since the break up of the Soviet Union will be one of the major challenges for Russia.

▶ Russian soldiers patrol a street in Grozny, Chechnya. There has been considerable tension and periodic violence between Russia and breakaway rebels who want an independent Chechnyan province. Overcoming the Chechnya issue is a major future challenge.

The Russian workforce also needs to adapt itself so that it is able to compete in an open and global economy.

Internationally Russia is gaining considerable status. In 2006 it held the presidency of the G8 (a group of the world's leading industrial nations) for the first time. Russia is also working towards becoming a member of the World Trade Organization (WTO), an international body that works to remove tariffs and other barriers to the free movement of capital, goods and services between countries. Russia is forming strong political ties with China and Japan, both of which are keen to access its vast energy reserves. It also maintains important political ties with Europe and the USA.

If Russia continues to recover at its present rate some experts believe it could quickly overtake Germany, France and the UK to become the largest economy in Europe. Its energy reserves are certainly vital to this, but in order to maintain its recovery the Russian economy will need to diversify into other sectors too. Russia also needs to reward more than the small cluster of elite entrepreneurs who appear to have gained most out of Russia's recent transformation. Post-Soviet Russia is by no means free of the problems it inherited upon independence, and it has acquired several new problems, too. With signs of progress and some significant trials behind them, however, many Russians view the future with considerable, and well-founded, optimism.

Timeline

2000 BC Early inhabitants settle in Russia.

c.500 AD Slavs occupy much of eastern Europe and what is now Russia.

c.850 Prince Rurik, a Viking trader, takes control of Slavs in Russia. Vikings form kingdom called Rus with its capital in Kiev (now in Ukraine).

c.982 Christianity arrives in Russia through trade links with Constantinople (now Istanbul in Turkey); it becomes the state religion in 988.

c.1237 Mongol Tatars led by Genghis Khan invade parts of Russia and gradually gain control of much of the country.

1447 Vasily II comes to power in Moscow and begins to consolidate his reign over other regions of Russia.

1613 Romanov family comes to power in Russia and begins a period of rule that lasts until 1917.

1861 Tsar Alexander II abolishes patterns of land ownership that have kept many Russians living as virtual serfs.

1881 Tsar Alexander II is killed by revolutionary terrorists, but they fail to overthrow the monarchy.

1894 Tsar Nicholas II comes to power following the death of his father Tsar Alexander III.

1915 Workers' strikes in protest at poor state of the economy.

1917 (January) Tsar Nicholas II instructs the army to disperse strikers in Moscow who are calling for the abolition of the monarchy, but army refuses and joins the strikers.

1917 (February) Tsar Nicholas II falls from power and flees to Tobolsk in north-western Russia.

1917 (October) Under Vladimir Lenin, the Bolshevik Party leads a revolution against the provisional government.

1917-22 Civil war between the Bolshevik 'Red Army' of Lenin and the armies of the ousted provisional government. Bolsheviks win the war.

1922 The USSR (Union of Soviet Socialist Republics) is formed.

1924 Lenin's death results in a power struggle for control of the USSR.

1928 Joseph Stalin comes to power as leader of the USSR.

1941 German forces invade the USSR during the Second World War.

1945 At the end of the Second World War, political differences between the USSR and its allies (UK, USA and France) lead to division that becomes known as the 'Cold War'.

1957 USSR succeeds in launching the first space satellite.

1961 USSR becomes the first nation to launch a manned space flight.

1985 Mikhail Gorbachev becomes leader in USSR and introduces reforms including *glasnost* and *perestroika*.

1986 A nuclear reactor at Chernobyl (now in Ukraine) explodes in the worst nuclear accident the world has known.

1991 (August) An attempted coup against Gorbachev is put down by President Yeltsin.

1991 (25 December) Gorbachev resigns.

1991 (31 December) The USSR ceases to exist.

1992 Russia emerges as new nation from the collapsed USSR with Boris Yeltsin as first president.

1994 Russian army enters Chechnya to reclaim control of breakaway republic.

1997 Ceasefire agreed between Russia and Chechnya.

1998 Russia joins the G7 (group of the world's seven wealthiest industrial nations) to form the G8.

1999 Fighting resumes between Russian forces and rebels in Chechnya.

1999 Yeltsin resigns as president and appoints his prime minister, Vladimir Putin as successor.

2002 (October) Chechen terrorists hold people hostage in a busy Moscow theatre.

2003 Referendum in Chechnya gives people there greater autonomy, but it remains part of Russia.

2004 (March) Putin is re-elected as president of Russia.

2004 (May) The new president of Chechnya, Akhmad Kadyrov, is murdered in a bomb attack.

2004 (September) Chechen terrorists hold a siege at a school in Beslan. The siege leaves 331 people dead.

2004 (November) Russia ratifies the Kyoto Protocol.

2006 Russia hosts the G8 summit in St Petersburg.

Glossary

Allied forces During the Second World War, the name given to the combined forces of Britain, France, the USA and the Soviet Union opposing Germany, Italy and Japan.

Bolshevik Party A communist revolutionary group led by Vladimir Lenin, which seized power in the 1917 revolution in Russia.

Chechen conflict A continuing war in the eastern part of the northern Caucasus in the south of Russia.

Communism/communist A social and political theory and system in which property and industry are owned by the state rather than by private business. A communist is a follower of communism.

Constitution A document that sets out the rights and duties of a government and its people.

Coup The overthrow of government by a group of people, usually using military force.

Deputy An elected representative in the parliament, who debates and votes on whether or not to pass laws. There are 450 deputies in the lower house of the Russian parliament and 178 in the upper house.

Ecology The study of the relationship of plants and animals to their environment.

Economy A community's system of using its resources to produce wealth.

Emigration The act of leaving one's own country to go to live permanently in another country.

Enclave A portion of territory surrounded by a larger territory. The people living in the enclave are often culturally and ethnically distinct from those in the larger territory.

Glasnost A policy of openness introduced by Mikhail Gorbachev in the Soviet Union in the mid-1980s.

Greenhouse gases Gases in the earth's atmosphere that are believed to trap heat from the sun and increase global warming.

Illiterate Unable to read or write.

Immigration The act of arriving to live permanently in a country that is not one's country of origin.

Inflation A fall in the value of money in terms of the amount of goods it can buy.

Kyoto Protocol An agreement made in 1997 in Kyoto, Japan, that requires developed countries to reduce their emissions of greenhouse gases by 2012 to an average of 5 per cent below levels in 1990.

Lichens Plants that grow as crusty patches or bushy growths on tree trunks and bare ground.

Literacy The ability to read and write.

Market economy A system in which individuals, rather than the state, make decisions about what to make and sell, based on and responding to what people want to buy.

NATO The North Atlantic Treaty Organization, an international organization made up of the USA, Canada and most European countries to guard international security.

Perestroika The restructuring of the Soviet state, a plan introduced by Gorbachev in the mid-1980s.

Republic A state in which power does not belong to a royal family but rather to an elected government.

Serfs Russian peasants who were considered to 'belong' to the person who owned the area in which they happened to be born.

Soviet Union The state founded after the Russian Revolution, run by the Communist Party and made up of 15 republics, with a population of 240 million and covering one-sixth of the world's land surface.

Steppes Vast, grassy plains.

Tsar The Russian emperor, and head of the Russian royal family.

World Heritage Site An area selected by a United Nations committee in the belief that it has particular value for the whole world and should be preserved.

Further Information

BOOKS TO READ

Eyewitness Guide: Russia
Kathleen Murrell
(Dorling Kindersley, 1998)

Days That Shook the World: The Russian Revolution
Paul Dowswell
(Hodder Children's Books, 2003)

Russia and the USSR: Empire and Revolution
Hamish Macdonald
(Longman, 2001)

A People's Tragedy: The Russian Revolution, 1891-1924
Orlando Figes
(Jonathan Cape, 1996)

Lands, Peoples & Cultures: Russia
Greg Nickles
(Crabtree Publishing Co., 2000)

Nations in Transition: Russia
Michael Kort
(Facts on File Inc, 2004)

Russia in the Modern World: A New Geography
Denis J. B. Shaw
(Blackwell, Oxford, 1999)

USEFUL WEBSITES

www.gov.ru/
The official website of the Russian government, providing information about all aspects of how the country is governed.

www.inside-russia.com/
A magazine-style site with articles and a newsletter about various aspects of modern Russia.

www.unicef.org/infobycountry/russia_29869.html
UNICEF website with country profile and statistics.

www.geographia.com/russia/

Official site of the Russian National Tourist Office, with information about history, art, major cities, and different regions.

www.ru/eng/index.html
A search engine called 'Russia on the Net', providing links to all aspects of Russian history, culture and current affairs.

http://uk.encarta.msn.com/encyclopedia_761569000_15/Russia.html
An excellent starting point for all information about Russia.

https://www.cia.gov/cia/publications/factbook/index.html
US government site providing up-to-date facts and figures about Russia.

www.greenpeace.org/russia/en/
The website of Greepeace in Russia, offering information about current environmental and conservation issues.

www.spartacus.schoolnet.co.uk
Educational website with an encyclopaedia on Russia, covering 1860-1945.

www.thecorner.org/hists/total/s-russia.htm &
http://www.historylearningsite.co.uk/russia_1917_to_1939.htm
Selections of articles on Soviet history 1917-39.

Index

Page numbers in **bold** indicate pictures.

About the Author

Rob Bowden is a freelance educational writer and photographer with a university background teaching geography and development studies. He has written and advised on many educational books and specializes in global environmental and social issues.

Born in Kirov in the former USSR, Galya Ransome is an experienced teacher of Russian at university, with a broad experience of interpreting and translating. She maintains a keen interest in developments in the post-Soviet era and visits Russia regularly. She has written and advised on many Russian books.